BLACK POEM

ALSO BY GARY COPELAND LILLEY

The Subsequent Blues
The Reprehensibles (chapbook)

BLACK POEM

A Chapbook

GARY COPELAND LILLEY

Hollyridge Press
Venice, California

© 2005 Gary Copeland Lilley

All rights reserved under International and Pan-American Copyright Conventions. Published in the United States by Hollyridge Press.

Hollyridge Press
P.O. Box 2872
Venice, California 90294
www.hollyridgepress.com

Cover and Book Design by Rio Smyth
Author Photo by Alan Kimrey
Manufactured in the United States of America by Lightning Source

ISBN-13: 978-0-9772298-1-9
ISBN-10: 0-9772298-1-5

Grateful acknowledgment is made to the editors of the publications in which the following poems first appeared:

Gargoyle: "The Dismal Swamp Just a Few Miles North of Home"
Greensboro Review: "Black Poem"
WPFW 89.3FM Poetry Anthology: "Funeral"

Contents

Black Poem	3
Gatesville, Joe Sears' Place	4
Charm City Tarot	5
Ranter On The Corner Of Babylon and Manhattan	15
Wahtuh	16
A Woman Wearing Red	17
Penitence at the All Local Calls Fifty Cents Confessional	18
Revival	20
November 11: Veterans' Day at Rite Liquor Store and Bar	22
My Mother Asks, Will it Kill Me?	23
Chicago Noir	25
American Rapture at 13 Degrees	27
It's About the Ponies	28
Diving to Test Depth on Watch Section 3	30
Funeral	31
The Temperature At Which Blood Flows	32
Solace	33
The Dismal Swamp Just a Few Miles North of Home	34

Black Poem

BLACK POEM

When I sat in back
Of Miss Ninth Grade Teacher's
Suppose to be remedial class
Courting Backrow Debbie
(Who I loved more than anything)
Ole teacher wanted us
To write poems on how we loves
And feels being black.

Now I ain't never seen
No black poem before
Because the books never say
Just what shade the thoughts were
And you never know what color
The poem-writer is
Unless they say so.

But my hand roam
All over Backrow Debbie.
Across her behind as soft
As the dandelions we'd picked
In the evening summer rains,
And I thought black
Must be something nice
To lay down in at night
And forget just how hard the day was.

GATESVILLE, JOE SEARS' PLACE

Where every wail and whoop
raises up roadhouse dust
and the one-arm proprietor
skins a smile and cuts a thick cigar
on the real teeth side of his mouth
expertly turning
his pistol hip away from the bar
pouring liquor fast
not spilling a drop and keeping
his bloodshot eye
on everyone.

CHARM CITY TAROT

1. King of Swords

I keep a sharpened knife; ain't got
my hand on no Glock looking
for no fool, got no cocked hot trigger
waiting on my pull. I'm old school,
driving my Hooptie-ville, playing
the cassette tape and fiending
for an eight-track, on north side B-More
turning out the lights with Teddy Pendergras.
Even in the part-truths you find salvations.
She can believe the wet-finger stories
caught in the hairs of her ear hole,
but she can not assume I've screwed
every woman in the phone book.

2. Three of Cups Reversed

In the parking lot she's washing her car,
bending down to wipe the rims.
Wide butt and showing waistline, always
some man wanting to wax her trunk.
Sitting on my back porch
in a lounger that's chained to the railing
I turn obstacles into stepping stones.
Dispel the negative and focus
on the self that hangs off my bones.
Beneath the ragged flag, the bare trees
in the spring, ashtray half full, fresh
pack of cigarettes and empty beer cans
on the small table at my side.

3. Justice

Reason looks good in boots; the bottle
blonde with body and brain mediates
and there are no disputes between us
important enough to mention.
Patient listening and even-handed
questions do more than enough
when the woman is talking
about not staying together
and everything is still cool.
I have to consider myself in concerns
of the heart, and have the final say
about when to leave the city.
I will have to leave the city.

4. The Hanged Man

I was a long night from being sober; napalm
retardant and smash proof, when I decided
to stop drinking, getting tattoos, and eating
fried food. Three fish popping in the skillet
on my stove, the scorned woman
hot sauce sitting on the shelf. And I gave up
smoking the non-menthol filter tips I've packed
around for thirty years. All my black clothes,
bundled dreadlocks, sacred antenna to God
that I'd cut from my head and offered to the fire.
I swore to sacrifice coffee beans, periodic migraines,
patchouli oil, and my left shoulder that creaks
when it gets cold in Baltimore.

5. Four of Swords

Personal history is the real root
of clarity, whose memory can I trust
but my own? The alley behind the house
is often better lit than the street.
Recall what was revealed inside the walls,
everyone adapts to change; the night guards
easing up as the day crew counts
before dawn , prophesy of the bars, spit shined
boots, small eyes, the knife scar
down the cheek of the sergeant, the smell
of coffee coming through the block,
spry young cons waiting on morning chow
talking about swaps of fatback for toast.

6. The Star

My first day on the mountain, a woman
sits with me on a porch swing, talking
about the voodoo gods getting into her
unfinished novel without her knowing,
and how the night before her car was full
of small white moths even though the windows
were closed. Then she speaks about having breast
reduction when she was 16 and I ask her
what size the girls are now. She just leans
them into me, saying she tells all her new lovers
about it because if they kiss along
the crease they'll see a trace of the knife
and may wrongly think of silicone.

7. Six of Wands Reversed

Ain't got the time for crazy shit,
put this pistol in your pocket
before we step. You get no bullets
because you're certain to trip
and shoot somebody and all we want
is the money. I'm going to keep
the loaded piece. I'm the better
shot and I'm going to look out for both
of us. No discussion. I have no love
for the penal system. This is the last time
I'm doing anything with you
and I don't want no blood,
I don't want no police.

8. Five of Pentacles

The foundation my grandmother built
squared the room, the Formica table,
a fifth of scotch for a centerpiece,
the spirits jumping into the conversation.
This was my Aunt Marcella's oracle
the day before she gave me a white car,
in the kitchen, pouring me a cup
in the last place I could call home.
Why, she asked me, do I always walk
in the hottest part of the day, and when
it comes to those hard deeds done free
by righteous people and martyrs,
isn't it time for that to be me?

9. Nine of Wands

I saw them again in the winter tonight,
wrapped in blankets, looking like Bedouins,
drop cloths and tarps billowing, a tent
over steam grates by the monument.
Their shopping carts parked like tourist buses,
a Polaroid. I live alone. As I drift to sleep
I rig for red, put the Jonah on a submarine
and I'm sitting on front steps, my woman
sensuous at the door screen in the twilight,
my mongrel pup rolling in the grass,
streetlamp shadows and teaser questions,
cool air that softly hums with the sound
of children playing chanting games.

10. Death

The black cat, someone had tossed
something on him, boiling water
or a chemical cleaner, hitting him along
the flank, leaving a large pale swatch
of bare skin. For two months he stalked
the alley slinking low and close
to the fences. But now he has new growth,
a darker patch in his coat, and he's in front
of the house, stretching and yawning
in the sun, spraying every bush in the yard
like this whole neighborhood belongs to him—
each chicken bone, all the bottle caps,
every female strutting her heat.

RANTER ON THE CORNER OF BABYLON AND MANHATTAN

I believe a little harder now GOD is readable the only distance learning international management is the city really safer in response watch please I lived for a reason war is grace staying alive and religious combat the art of the dead honoring ether for political paralysis the prairie found a charmed life I am not in a dream sequence amazing sidewalk spirits what you can do GOD you got the Sunday 357 you got the edge walking famous leap year babies all God's children got found traditions and bushels of burning chads look how they run amuck in front of God's annoyed hands freaks and space treats with eight stomping feet venture for I believe in good the deep GOD the lifeline the silver sands day jams favorite things and an empty house is furnished jumble painless GOD zone jumble painless GOD zone better heard than seen the truth moment side effects payoffs I got history on a deadline I got hell fear on ice please visit the attacks don't leave without the word listen to your cell phone tell me whose voice it was called our heroes home GOD almighty violence death is your duct tape stop stop the devil's in a fury condom nation GOD the whole world of Gonzo gives a memorial then take a closer look and a date is the date the stakes the many avenues of animal care at the wreckage watching GOD points your coke-filled nose to real opportunity ground zero rushed-out schemes the damned the look-alikes foam boxes choke the site breathe vaporized people my strict policy is ask your doctor it is the beginning this power that haunts the hard knock we have with Godfather green pastures that vary we are lost again with our global tracking lost again hope going and nothing feels certain but GOD you are called my bigger engine my bigger nigga business first class mail idol a reply to the rest the rubble the rabble unlucky ghosts in the tower of babble this mocked world still reeks of bravado but jet-fuel lights when GOD has left the building.

WAHTUH

A summer storm shot across my luck,
the machine voice, the flat palm of a woman
on weed, motor oil, and persistent rumors.
To cool my ear I'll need a river.
Such a mean sky, a dizzy lick,
a thrill time garden of ricochets,
that ecstatic carnival urge, her gracious giggle
when we leave the road through a tunnel of trees
on Johns Island, South Carolina.
Longing to be a good night tingle lizard
hitting thermal shots straight up,
I drive through her rain and mud
then we're holding close on a porch rocker,
she's sliding back and forth into her Gullah.

A WOMAN WEARING RED

So I picked up the obscene call on the white courtesy phone and asked the party for the number so I could call her back from the hotel room, and it was a 1-900 number, which I don't mind, cause everybody got to eat, and then I remembered this escort gal in Charleston, she wore Shangri-La dresses, and had a black heart-of-thorns tattoo on her bicep, and it's possible I may have loved her about a hundred years, from the moment she told me she poured some very heavy whiskey and then showed me that she did, and she always said I should taste her home fries which I have not yet experienced in any of her mornings, but I believe she's righteous she looks like the whole truth, and nothing but a real good and necessary lie would ever come from her mouth, yes, she had a pretty sweet purr and the right shoes to show her pretty heels, rode a pair of mules to get your attention, the kind of woman who could drive you home even when she's drunk, the gal you look for if you're coming down a ragged pier after being under the sea for a few months, and whatever God you have grants you some mercy, oh yes, you have to have the faith that she's there, in all her pleasant homespun profanities, to bring some damn grace to your sad sailor life, and you know that she will notice all of your sutures, all your contusions, and won't ask 'til it's private because she's polite and near perfect in her pathological ways, so I went down the thread-bare hall to my dingy room with the window nailed shut and sat down with yesterday's news, reading the not-so-funnies, wondering how did she know where to find me.

PENITENCE AT THE ALL LOCAL CALLS FIFTY CENTS CONFESSIONAL

I'm wearing black, with my dreadlocks flying,
a duffle bag of poet clothes. My sister, Ruby,
does not pick up the call. The gang boys
are riding bicycles around the payphone.
I ain't leaving unless things get rough,
and I ain't looking for the law. I rode the train
four days to get here. How do I start?
I gave my mother a gun, a Smith and Wesson
Combat .22 Magnum with a nine shot cylinder
and a heavy frame. The extra weight
made for balance, accuracy. That pistol
was a good fit for her hand. My mother
never married my father but she's been married
two times since. Her second husband, Simon,
the preacher's brother, got upset because I didn't act
like I needed his permission to be in the house.
He's just my mother's husband. I pulled out
a bottle of Jack and drank it by myself
sitting in my mother's kitchen. He quit his job
and burned my mother's house down.
Tossed a molotov from the yard, got into the Ford
she'd help pay for and drove off. The folks
on Lowground Road say he was driving
like he'd set himself on fire. My mother lived
on her brother's farm while she cleared the plot
for a double-wide trailer. That's why you don't
see pictures of us as kids, no certificates
for perfect attendance, no trophies, no awards.

Then last week Simon came back. I didn't expect
to find him laying in my mother's living room,
shot with my registered gun. Everything burns.
Am I to blame for fire? Because of him
there's not one document to prove
me and Ruby even had childhoods, and now
I keep getting her answer machine.

REVIVAL

On the moaner's bench
some old folks every Sunday
in a storefront of red brick.
Today is worship

and security bars are pulled back.
A black industrial door
with hand-lettered name and address
of the First Missionary Baptist Church.

Half-way down the block a boy
in a big coat assumes the position
by the currency exchange that'll cash
your check and tax you for the privilege

like they're the United States government.
The old folks shake tambourines, stomp
the floor, make their bodies into drums.
Someone opens a song carried for years

in a pocket all the way from the fields.
There's a liquor store, and the Palestinians
owners are afraid in this country now.
This is their turn as aliens of the hour.

Their sons hip-hop like us and work
the Sabbath. Open 18 hours a day.
A crowd lines up for the sacraments
kept behind bulletproof glass;

the booze, the lottery, the cigarettes,
the condoms, candy, and Similac.

The Arabs say they're businessmen
and can't understand why we don't know

in this country about the blood-value of oil.
At the bus stop the hustlers work
beneath a camera that never captures
their images, they believe in the holy stash

of rocks in a balled-up bag.
The narcotics lay beside the garbage can.
The old folks ask the church's blessing
for those sick and afflicted, ask salvation

for their children and grandkids
who are not in attendance, but today
there's proof the devil is losing, sirens
can not be heard inside hallelujah.

NOVEMBER 11: VETERANS' DAY AT RITE LIQUOR STORE AND BAR

Division Street. Nothing like a bit of booze, blues,
and a televised parade to put doom on the horizon.
The owner is politely telling Jose about the boy,
"To me, he is nothing, but he is your son
and you are my friend. Tell him stay out of here
with those gang-bangers. Okay?" Lopez, another
Vietnam vet, pontificates about the mercy involved
in the act of shooting again an enemy combatant
mortally wounded. That's when Mike, who sits
at the end of the bar, asks Lopez the question.
"Hey Loco, " he says, "if I give you a million dollars
would you do some mercy to this." He grabs hold
of himself. Lopez fires back instantly, "For a million
I'll do anything you want, you buy me a drink
right now and then we'll talk." The whole dark bar,
about six of us sailors and grunts absolutely crack up.
A gut laugh right in the midst of whatever memories
we have of all those who've died in the boonies
and died on the roads. Angel, in desert chocolate chips
and tattoos, a veteran of the Gulf says, "Are you
listening, Mike? I'll even shave for that million bucks."
Then Carla, an ex-Marine, jumps in, "Forget all that,
I'll do it right now for a hundred, and you better be fast
because I ain't on no mission. If you want the mission,
Mike, you'll have to give me the whole million."
And now even Jose is picking up his shot and we're
all bent over squench-eyed knocking our beers
against the bar, everyone laughing hard, alive
and watching Mike go through his pockets.

MY MOTHER ASKS, WILL IT KILL ME?

I'm claustrophobic. I've made
eight submarine patrols
and this was a truth I knew
after the first four. I won't live
in a basement apartment. I find
no comfort under low ceilings.
At sea if I went more than two weeks
without sleep the Doc would give me pills
that would let me sleep and wake up
alert enough to respond to alarms,
casualties, and drills.
I can't stand being contained.
I told my family I don't want to be buried.
Consider that I'll have consciousness
after death, in a coffin.
I know how steel sounds under pressure.
I know what depth it begins to sing.
There are valleys at sea, deep enough
to crush us, the ship gives a tone,
a hum when the hull starts to compress.
You think you're seeing the plates move.
It starts low but the whining of steel
gets louder as a submarine dives.
I want, I say, to be cremated.
Name someone else in this family
besides you, my mother says,
who'd choose to be in hell twice.
It's ashes that will inherit the earth.
A scattering of ashes? That's an odd fit
for this family's funerals,
someone leaves we lay the body
beneath their stone.

We're in the church cemetery
on Lowground Road
and I'd just poured libation
at the roots of our evergreen.
The family plots are in its shade.
I know she's right, I belong
with them, in this purgatory
of a hole in the ground.

CHICAGO NOIR

—Blues tribute to Motherwell

Western Ave: leaving the blue line
I can't name the tune
the National Steel guitar and street traffic
are playing but I remember dancing to it.
Her hip, right side, the near back,
above the waistline a tattoo
of black ink; the shoot of irises
I've held in my hands.

A man doesn't know anything
until he's breathed air at least 30 years—
what he's knows then
is that he knows nothing. I am not
the priest of the modern drama
but I can tell you every mistake
I think I've made. My qualified heart
has been going off like a car alarm.

Doctor Feelgood says I may get better,
baby, he's just not sure I'll ever be well.
I thought this alluring woman was gone.
Gave her logical reasons to leave
a middle-age man. The concern,
she's almost too-much younger,
a million shades of blues have been sung
about being in such a situation.

In the dim golden light of Rosa's club,
during the whiskey solo and compliments
of cigar smoke and harmonica,

I lean towards her. She's been waiting
for this and comes to meet me.
The amazing glory of the now,
her sensuous mouth proves—
the prime rule of love is don't be dead.

AMERICAN RAPTURE AT 13 DEGREES

Me and my boy are at the wild-card game,
only time I've been in a stadium.
The boss at one of the buildings I clean
gave me 2 tickets, so we're not watching
TV we are in it, close to the field
in the north end zone seats. Our guys score
the winning touchdown on a shuffle pass,
and coming toward us, giving the ball
to my son is the player who'd slanted
inside untouched. You could see every nick
and paint scrape on the helmet, and my boy
is jumping and screaming. The noise
of the frost-bit crowd can not drown him out,
his passion fills me like I have 2 hearts.

IT'S ABOUT THE PONIES

I'm at the racetrack with Zoot
and we're both drinking coffee now
because the bourbon has us down
and he doesn't like how I bet
so I make the run and buy us
two large goddamn Styrofoam cups.
I take the long shots black with sugar
he reads the racing forms
and tracks how the local horses ran
the last four Fridays at Pimlico.
He contends good horses only lose
when the jockeys stop whipping them
so he digs slap-happy drivers and always
checks to see who's holding the reins
and I say I like my horses smiling.
Plus he's wearing his racetrack clothes
a slick-as-shit blue pin-stripe suit
and his Tio's gray fedora that he stole
while paying respect at the wake.
Got on a pair of one size too small
highly-glossed blue alligator knobs
he found in a thrift shop in New Orleans.
He puts the polish on himself
because he's too tight-fist
to pay someone else to shine them.
And here I am in black wrangler jeans
a cotton shirt with holes in the sleeves
looking like the all-day sucker
but a hundred bucks to the good.
It's obvious he doesn't like my smile
and when I try to make small talk
he says if I can't shut my mouth
I might as well just change my seat.

You'd think I'd said something bad
about John Coltrane who's on
a gold medallion dangling off his neck
like it's some type of racetrack crucifix.
He's chewed down to the last three inches
of his Cuban cigar his left eye
half-closed in the stogie smoke
that creeps up the side of his face.
He's a man of bad habits and he's as mad
as the first wife of a bigamist
because I've won more money than him.
He's a riot sipping his black coffee quiet
while keeping his half-eye off me
and that's the shit that has me worried
because he might not drive me home
on account of my gambling approach
lacking horse logic or player sense.
He gets pissed when he discovers
I'm a sorry ass who can't remember
the damn horse's name
and his left eye slams shut in disgust
the cigar stub glows on one side
of the mouth while he spits
from the other telling me
that I'd won the money
in the third race with El Diablo
on the ride whipping pure hell
out of Lucky's Paradise.

DIVING TO TEST DEPTH ON WATCH SECTION 3

Lester Yates, your blow-up doll
should have stayed in port.
There is no certifiable evidence
of you abusing her in any way;
we are tired of seeing your date
in front of the scheduled flick,
and sitting in the crew's mess
when we're eating chow,
the gapped washable mouth
and her dead green eyes
spoiling every fantasy in our heads.
We have taken and deflated her,
if you expect to see your friend again
you will do exactly as we say.
If you buck against anything
we will send you some of her pieces.
You are to leave 3 packs of cigarettes,
different brands, one of which
will be menthol, by the anchor housed
indicator. You will walk this submarine
from torpedo tubes aft through control,
missile mid-level, past the reactor
into the engine room, and wait
at the shaft, wearing nothing
but skivvies and a dosimeter.
We will contact you there
with further instructions.

FUNERAL

—for Michael Andrew Lilley

Through tight brick towns
across asphalt beaches
my heart weedy and littered
roadwide pain hounding
whore highways north
like a prophet proven false
by the news of your death.

Deliver us sweet Christ

I have broke bread
with whoever was hungry
and now I pray for you
crossing the state lines.

When our feet of stone stumble

A loaded weapon
and I sweat the fever
my hands tremble
like demons and I thirst
one bourbon my savior
in this death damned dawn.

And the soul is a sack of sand.

I have improvised a fitful bed
along the obscene wall I have
not slept in this dead house
boarded up and bare inside.
I hear your moon-calling
footsteps scratch and crow
like a rooster on a sidewalk.

THE TEMPERATURE AT WHICH BLOOD FLOWS

I toss a dash of salt in my pot of coffee
      to settle the grounds

by now I suppose he's at that woodpile
      the personal

question that my family does not ask
      my mother is

so proud he's the first grandson
      to do this/

walk a mile to her and split armloads
      of oak sticks

and kindling every evening this boy
      almost tall as I am

the man of this house and lord
      without trying to

I get mad because he's no mirror I don't
      see myself any

where in him every morning I pray
      remove what pain

comes between us/he works the axe
      'til light fades

gathers the chips in a pail and he goes in
      to my mother's kitchen

where they'll have their cups and talk
      close to the stove.

SOLACE

It doesn't cost anything to get high on your hopes. My grandfather never filled up his car, claimed every vehicle he ever drove only broke down with a full tank of gas. I haven't worked in a month and the note is due. Phone bill's on the table beside the water and cable. I don't even look up anymore when the lights start to flicker like Stella Blue, who I met at a rent party of at Joe Beasley's third floor loft. She was dancing by herself to bass and drum. A tall woman, wearing long black boots, tight black jeans, and nothing else but a black bra. Not a laundry type of bra, but one of Victoria's nothing-is-secret bras. A black lacy arrangement. It looked like roses were climbing up her trellises, so I stepped towards her. Months later she's telling me how amazed she is that everything is going so fast and so good between us. She thinks back to the night we met and asks what made me approach her. I say, the small lace roses coming across your tits. And Stella Blue didn't like that one bit. She walked out, and I went drinking at a round of bars. I get her at last call and she's on the dance floor half-naked with some other dude. I toss down my drink, peel the hell right out the place, past the police car parked idling down the street. For some reason I turn the radio on and a Bible-belt gospel starts spilling like a prophesy, a consideration for migration to some storefront Detroit church filled with halleluiahs, because this is the moment when I recognize that I need me a prayer, a rolling sermon for the Blues God, just one sweaty song, please sisters, about troubles not lasting always.

THE DISMAL SWAMP JUST A FEW MILES NORTH OF HOME

Ain't gotta go where you was,
that's my aunt's advice to me
when she gave me the keys
to the white '87 Cutlass Supreme.
Ten years of her dents, and no reverse.
I drove to DC from Sandy Cross,
along the edge of The Dismal Swamp
where I used to go to get away
from the shattering of the house.

It's about truth. He said
he recognized the face he saw in me.
I would pull off the blacktop
up to the muck and water,
into the natural silences caught
in the twisted roots of cypress
to smoke and plan on the burning
of this man with my bootleg hoodoo,
to stir piss and swamp water
into his ashes.

Friday nights his truck cooling
in the yard, he sits in the house
until he's drunk enough to cause us
to hide the gun. "Tell Mama,"
some road memory on the radio,
high-beam on the Spanish moss,
the beatings would run through
the weekend. A Sunday deacon,
my mother refuses make-up
and she sits in church in dark shades,
as he prays for someone, maybe
Etta James, to make
everything alright.

www.ingramcontent.com/pod-product-compliance
Lightning Source LLC
Chambersburg PA
CBHW022346040426
42449CB00006B/738